Masks and Measures

Verses From A Viral Time

Rajeev Kumar Dubey

New Delhi • London

BLUEROSE PUBLISHERS
India | U.K.

Copyright © Rajeev Kumar Dubey 2025

All rights reserved by author. No part of this publication may be reproduced, stored in a retrieval system or transmitted in any form or by any means, electronic, mechanical, photocopying, recording or otherwise, without the prior permission of the author. Although every precaution has been taken to verify the accuracy of the information contained herein, the publisher assumes no responsibility for any errors or omissions. No liability is assumed for damages that may result from the use of information contained within.

BlueRose Publishers takes no responsibility for any damages, losses, or liabilities that may arise from the use or misuse of the information, products, or services provided in this publication.

For permissions requests or inquiries regarding this publication, please contact:

BLUEROSE PUBLISHERS
www.BlueRoseONE.com
info@bluerosepublishers.com
+91 8882 898 898
+4407342408967

ISBN: 978-93-6452-981-5

Cover Design: Aman Sharma
Typesetting: Pooja Sharma

First Edition: January 2025

About the Poet

Rajeev Kumar Dubey is currently working as a Professor of Anaesthesiology at the Institute of Medical Sciences, Banaras Hindu University, Varanasi (India). His academic background comprises the disciplines of Anaesthesiology, Critical care, Psychological Counselling and Hospital Administration. Apart from being a popular teacher and eminent physician, he is also a candid author and a sensitive poet.

The book "Masks and Measures" is rooted in the backdrop of the current global COVID-19 pandemic. It has been written mainly to promote a healthy lifestyle, raise public awareness, and salute the brave warriors fighting against the corona virus. Amid the unbearable pain brought by COVID-19, this poetry collection sparks new hope and energy in the heart. Each piece in the collection sounds the trumpet of inevitable victory over the pandemic.

From the start of the COVID crisis, the poet has been deeply involved in treating patients in the ICU and handling administrative duties. Through these experiences, he has felt the cries of humanity with immense sensitivity. These poems, born from the poet's empathy and the doctor's unwavering confidence, offer comfort and provide a clear and positive vision of the future. By highlighting the importance of COVID-appropriate behaviour and a scientific approach, the poet brings a fresh perspective to ancient Indian culture, spirituality, Raja Yoga, and human values.

***

Prologue

In the 21st century, science and technology have blessed the world with countless comforts but have also brought troubles. Just as the proud human race was battling these challenges, a terrifying pandemic suddenly shook the world. All those deadly weapons that humanity had created were rendered useless, as a tiny corona virus brought the whole planet to its knees. Feeling unsafe, people hid away in their homes. No one had any idea how deadly this silent enemy would be. In the blink of an eye, it claimed millions of lives. It threw the social systems into chaos, jobs vanished, and the economy crumbled. The fast-paced world, which had been soaring ahead, ended abruptly. Everyone was left helpless, silent, and stunned.

From rulers and administrators to teachers, trainers, writers, journalists, and ordinary people—everyone jumped into this great battle against corona virus. This collection of poems, Masks and Measures, offers a glimpse into those times and inspires humanity to look within. When a teacher, poet, and doctor merge into one, something truly unique is born—like the creations of Dr Rajeev. This collection brings together the sensitive poet, the brave warrior doctor, and the empowering teacher—all rolled into one person. It is as if Dr Rajeev is trying to revive a world that has been stunned by the poisonous rain of the corona virus with the life-giving rain of his creativity. Describing immediate measures to fight the pandemic, this selection of poems portrays Dr Rajeev as a true friend of humanity.

Creating an entire poetry collection on 'Corona virus' shows how compassionate the poet is. The virus deeply stirred the poet's heart to reflect and work on it. His gentle heart cares about people, blending the compassion of Buddha with the strength of Krishna. The poet's works inspire us to adapt our way of life to make the future bright.

The world's suffering moves the poet's tender heart. The doctors emerge as warriors, ready to sacrifice themselves to protect human life. By saying, "These tough days will pass; we will overcome Corona one day," the poet highlights the unbeatable human spirit. With the lines, "If there's a problem, there will be a solution; if the night is dark, the dawn will come," he has tried to fill the world with positive energy. To ensure that 'social distancing' does not create confusion, the poet emphasises, "Keep social distance but do not let there be any separation in our hearts. No town or village should be left unprotected from Corona." The poet encourages every town and village to stay connected with their hearts. By stating, "Adhere to social distancing, wash hands with water and soap, and wear a mask daily—these are the three main things to remember," the poet offers a simple mantra for defeating Corona.

The poet's strong desire to tackle Corona from all angles and eradicate it is compelling. The world will surely overcome this crisis, and the poet's wish will undoubtedly come true. These works of the poet are destined to be timeless. I extend my heartfelt congratulations to Dr Rajeev for completing this collection. This compilation will surely achieve its purpose and benefit the readers.

Congratulations on this Herculean effort! Best wishes!

Dated: December 15, 2024   ***Anand Shekhar Upadhyay***

                                         Mount Abu, Rajasthan

***

Contents

A Sacred Offering 1

Serene Surrender 4

Tips for Keeping Safe 5

Faith and Patience 6

Patience 7

Awareness 8

Reflections 9

Safety Ring 11

War 13

Etiquette 15

Crimson Dawn 16

Virus 17

Man-At-Arms 19

Musk 21

Distance 22

The Nation Will Fight 23

Alert 25

Seriousness 26

Victory Will Be Ours 27

Dignity 28

Iqbal 29

The Warriors	31
Duty	32
Responsibility	33
Empathy	34
A Tale of Sanjeevani and Despair	36
Identity	38
Vital Air	39
Examination	40
A Wake-Up Call	41
In Accord	42
Courage	44
Triumph through Adversity	45
Dark Days	47
Gift of Fearlessness	49
Sacrifices for Safety	50
Healing	52
Empowered Triumph	54
Blessed Guardians	56
Awakening Awareness	57
Eid of Hope	58
Heavenly Triumph	59
Battle of Resolve	61
Vaccination	63
Slaves to Our Own Delusions	65
Fear	66

Victory Call 67
Navigating Crisis with Grace 69
Epiphany 70
Witness 72
Salutation 73

A Sacred Offering

Dear readers!
This offering is plain–
A collection of "Masks and Measures" is for you again.
With deep respect,
This gift I place–
In your hands, may it find its grace!

Corona spreads,
A fierce tide–
But even this has reasons we cannot hide.
With a calm heart,
Seek truth, explore–
Let us dive within for self-restore.

Let life be calm,
And let discipline reign–
In words and deeds, let purpose remain.
Eat what is right,
Sleep and wake–
Balanced living is a pledge we make.

Two yards apart,
Masks on the face–
Embrace this new life with grace.
Wash hands frequently,
Live pure and bright–
Let yoga spread its guiding light.

Let the nature, our friend,
Be no longer afraid–
Let us protect it, a vow to be made.
Plant more trees,
Clean the air–
Keep the earth fertile, pure, and fair.

Let fresh air flow
And rivers stay clear–
Make every bit of earth dear.
A healthy body,
And a fearless mind–
Let freedom be the path we find.

The disease is brutal,
Cures are few–
Vaccines have come into view.
Stay alert,
Victory will come–
A new example will strike the drum.

Our resolve is firm,
Our victory is certain,
The pandemic, we can contain.
Leading us forth
May every wish find its way!
Guided by India's spiritual ray.

December 15, 2024 ***Rajeev Kumar Dubey***
Professor, Department of Anesthesiology
Institute of Medical Sciences
Banaras Hindu University, Varanasi

***

Serene Surrender

The brave doctors—
Till their final breath,
They serve tirelessly, defying death.
Steadfast in their resolve,
Fearless they stand—
True symbols of humanity's hand.

Leaving home behind,
Awake day and night—
Living a life of ascetic light.
Lips sealed in silence,
Tears on the brink—
Boundless as the sky, free as we think.

A million salutes,
With flowers of love—
To you, Warriors! Sent from above.
When you walk this earth,
As gods nearby—
Even death must pass you by.

***

Tips for Keeping Safe

In cities and towns, near or far away,
Here is the word on keeping Corona at bay.

Observe the advice as it expands—
Do not touch your eyes, and wash your hands.

Keep your fingers clear,
Mask up your face, from ear to ear.

Stay apart, do keep some space,
Information is your shield in this murky race.

These are the tips to stay in the clear,
Follow them carefully, and hold close your loved and dear.

***

Faith and Patience

Always clean your hands,
Wear a mask in place,
Keep six feet apart,
Give each other a space.

These are the mantras we all must heed,
For everyone's safety, these are the steps we need.
Clean hands, masks on, six feet away,
Let's win this battle and make the virus sway.

No slackening now; every step is the key,
Missing even one could leave us at sea.
With faith and patience, we will rise to the call,
Face each challenge, and stand tall through it all.

With the wisdom and courage to spare,
We will turn this tide and show we care.
Clean hands, masks on, six feet apart,
These mantras will guide us straight from the heart.

***

Patience

COVID will surely fade; hold on a bit more,
Do not let carelessness or slackness take over the floor.
Wearing masks and keeping a distance is the best shield,
With patience and persistence, victory will be revealed.

Stick to two yards until proper medicine is in sight,
COVID will surely fade; hold on tight.
Do not let carelessness or slackness find a way,
Keep your focus sharp every single day.

Offices and shops are open, business is back in gear,
COVID is still around, so be clear.
Stay alert, continue your work with care,
Do not let carelessness or slackness slip into your air.

COVID will surely fade; no need to despair.

***

Awareness

COVID is still around, so do not let your guard down,
Two yards apart, masks are a must—
Beware of any breach of trust.

There is no cure or vaccine for the illness we face,
Let us keep life on track with joy and grace.
Just a bit of vigilance and safety embrace,
Will keep misfortune at bay in every place.
Two yards apart, masks are a must—
Beware of any act of disgust.

[Note: As of the date of writing, the vaccine was not yet available.]

***

Reflections

There is no cure yet for COVID, hope we rely on,
Victory is possible with two yards, as we have drawn.
When stepping out, always mask your face,
Wash hands with soap in the first place.

Our final mistake, a chance we will not get,
Victory is within reach, provided we do not forget.
Hindu, Muslim, Sikh, or Christian,
Rich or poor are not a partition.

We are Indians first, united in the fight.
If one link weakens, our defeat is in sight.
Be it any state or zone, street or highway, in or out,
COVID must not intrude after the measures we take stout.

Virus is the friend of none— child, youth or old,
With two yards apart, we stay safe manifold.
We have conquered many diseases before,
And with generations past, we have endured more.

Let us prepare together, like the churning of the sea,
Victory is in our grasp if we agree.
Two yards apart, masks in place,
Together, we will conquer and win this race.

***

Safety Ring

Let us practice social distancing,
Do not break the safety ring.

A global pandemic is here,
No cure for COVID is there.
Understand the depth of the plight,
Add safety measures to the fight.
Let us practice social distancing,
Do not break the safety ring.

Do not touch your eyes carelessly,
Wash your hands with soap regularly.
Put the mask on your face–
Quit alcohol and tobacco that bring disgrace.
Let us practice social distancing,
Do not break the safety ring.

COVID is still an enigma,
Be responsible to break the stigma.
Understand the golden tool–
Responsibility is the safety rule.

Whether at home or office, or on the street,
Always be vigilant and stay discreet.
Let us practice social distancing,
Do not break the safety ring.

***

War

We shall honour the chain of protection,
Never let our guard drop, with dedication.

Friends! Join, extend your hand,
Together, we will rise and make a stand.
Keep two yards apart,
We will fight COVID with courage in the heart.

Clean hands with soap every day,
Keep your mask on, come what may.
Get tested if you have any fear.
Do not hesitate; the path is clear.

Friends! Join, extend your hand,
Together, we will rise and make a stand.
Keep two yards apart,
We will fight COVID with courage in the heart.

Face the disease, unemployment too,
Hunger and hardship—see them through.

With preparation and responsible action,
We will paint a new dawn with unwavering passion.

Friends! Join, extend your hand,
Together, we will rise and make a stand.
Keep two yards apart,
We will fight COVID with courage in the heart.

***

Etiquette

No cure, no remedy—
For COVID, as of today.

An unsolved puzzle remained—
Many deep secrets are still unexplained.

Two yards apart, masks are a must,
Stay aware as a collective trust.

Maintain social distancing all the time—
Be it prayer or any daily rhyme.

A new way to live, we have been shown,
Nature has blessed us, and our path is now known.

***

Crimson Dawn

A two-yard distance, a mask put tight—
It will make us win this fight.
Neither the battle is over yet,
Nor is there any cure for this threat.

It is unfair to relax even for a bit—
Whether in the office, field or grit.
A two-yard distance, a mask put tight—
It will make us win this fight.

Wearing the mask properly,
Observe social distancing diligently.
Let us light up the dismal night,
And bring a crimson dawn so bright.

A two-yard distance, a mask put tight—
It will make us win this fight.

***

Virus

A virus eloped from the land of China,
Its name is "Corona."
Now, it has spread across the planet,
Deluging every corner and facet.

Do not be careless anymore,
Fight it with prudence to settle the score.
Always wear your mask with care,
And wash your hands, beware!
A virus eloped from the land of China,
Its name is "Corona."

Avoid crowded places, stay apart,
And keep a two-yard distance from the start.
Prevention is the only cure,
That no magic or medicine can ensure.
A virus eloped from the land of China,
Its name is "Corona."

When you come home from outside–
Whether from the shop or office side,
Soak your clothes for thirty minutes straight,
In soap and water, do not hesitate.
A virus eloped from the land of China,
Its name is "Corona."

Eat healthy and stay clean,
Sleep on time; turn off the screen.
Say goodbye to tobacco and betel,
Practice yoga, breathe deep, and settle.
A virus eloped from the land of China,
Its name is "Corona."

Wage a war against the malady,
Medicines and vaccines will soon be ready.
Strengthen your immunity
To plant the seed of victory.
A virus eloped from the land of China,
Its name is "Corona."

***

Man-At-Arms

Salute to the warriors of Corona—
We honour them with deep respect.
Who gave their body, mind and soul,
And their wealth and lives for us to protect.

Days, weeks, and months have elapsed,
They stayed away from home, unsurpassed.
Though we may not survive this fight,
Humanity must endure the night.
Salute to the warriors of Corona—
We honour them with deep respect.

They did not think of family or throne,
In this battle, they stood alone.
Salute to the warriors of Corona—
We honour them with deep respect.

Let us shower them with flowers and grace—
With love in the heart and a smiling face.
Light up every home with festive lights,
In honour of their endless fights.

Salute to the warriors of Corona—
We honour them with deep respect.

From sky to earth, with clapping hands,
And a united heart that understands—
Though kept apart, our bond is clear;
Let us lift our nation and spread the cheer.
Salute to the warriors of Corona—
We honour them with deep respect.

We honour the warriors in this fray
With a heartfelt hug from two steps away.
Salute to the warriors of Corona—
We honour them with deep respect.

***

Musk

Keeping two steps apart is crucial,
As the Corona's wrath is real.

Follow the rules with care,
Only then will your journey be fair.

Prevention is the key
When treatment is not easy.

The sky, the earth and the breeze serene
Make us feel even more pristine.

Time will pass,
And the morning will be bright.
The fragrant feelings of the heart
Will bloom like musk, pure and light.

***

Distance

Let there be social distance but no distance in the heart,
Let our towns and villages become COVID-smart.

With balanced food and balanced living,
Proper sleep and waking, giving.
Disease is impossible when nature is in harmony;
When the environment is pure, life is a symphony.
In a disciplined life, let there be no lack of restraint,
Let there be social distance but no bitterness or complaint.

It is a tricky problem but with a simple solution—
Hand washing with soap and water prevents dissemination.
There is no pandemic so strong
That we cannot find a way to get along.
Let there be social distance but no distance in our hearts,
Every challenge has a remedy, where healing starts.

***

The Nation Will Fight

The nation will fight,
We will not sit idle with our hands in our lap—
We will battle this disease, the Corona trap.

Whoever we are in this regard—
A homemaker, a border guard,
A labourer, a sanitation worker,
A farmer from the village or a city dweller.
In tough times, we will unitedly fight with determination,
Fully prepared, not sitting idle with resignation.

Scientists and doctors are joining forces,
To conquer the pandemic with their resources.
Agriculture, service, and industry—
Let the wheel of progress run free.
May farmers and workers not suffer
From hunger, pain, or forced labour.
We will not sit idle with our hands in our lap—
In the time of crisis, we will not take a nap.

The eyes of the world are on us now,
In despair, it looks to India somehow.
Any question that arises,
The solution, the holy Gita advises.
Through sacrifice, we overcome every disaster,
We will not sit idle but create destiny as a master.

***

Alert

There is no need to fear,
Just stay a bit alert and clear.
Battle with COVID is not benign,
Let our minds, words and actions align.

Social distancing need not flatter,
Wash hands with soap and water,
Wear your mask without fail–
These are the three main rules to prevail.
Battle with COVID is not benign,
Let our minds, words and actions align.

***

Seriousness

With a courage that knows no breach,
Victory is never out of reach.
After the darkest night,
A bright day is always in sight.

Through social distancing,
We will achieve triumph in the ring.
A determination steadfast
Makes the success everlast.

***

Victory Will Be Ours

We will be victorious.
Every pandemic can be caged,
Just stay alert and conscious.
We will be victorious.

Keep away from the jostling throng,
Stay at home, safe and strong.
Let the infection rate decrease,
And the misleading rumours cease.
Social distancing is precious.
We will be victorious.

***

Dignity

The vaccine has arrived; congratulations to all,
But let us remain strict and heed the call.
Do not slack off on discipline; be stern,
Wearing masks and keeping a safe distance are still of concern.

Maintain some dignity in life,
Simple living and modest diet, free from strife.
Shun imitation, embrace nature,
Balanced living is indeed a treasure.

With the steadfast mind eternal,
Let us limit our needs and be frugal.
Whether it is agriculture or labour,
The pandemic, we shall conquer.

Life shall bloom from dawn to dusk
With the aroma of musk.

***

Iqbal

The battle with Corona is still ongoing,
But together, we will win—our turn is showing.

Take care of yourself, let the hard times pass,
Regret nothing, and let no such actions trespass.
Change the way we live—
Let the wisdom be cohesive.
The battle with Corona is still ongoing,
But together, we will win—our turn is showing.

The situation will change, and we will make it right,
With an unparalleled courage, shining bright.
We will provide the necessary intervention,
No path will be narrow, and all preparations are in action.
The battle with Corona is still ongoing,
But together, we will win—our turn is showing.

Let our resolve be firm for the noble cause,
May the world be amazed by our unyielding applause.
The disease may confine us, but we will stand tall;
Together, we will overcome it all.
The battle with Corona is still ongoing,
But together, we will win—our turn is showing.

***

The Warriors

On the path of duty,
And the chariot of victory—
The Corona warriors stand strong.
With life at stake,
Do make no mistake—
Let us combat COVID all along.

Leaving home and hearth behind,
As descendants of Charaka, aligned—
We march ahead with pride.
Serving with utmost dedication,
No medal, wealth or position
Can dampen our stride.

Wear your masks,
Avoid any lapses in tasks—
O brothers and sisters! Our victory is certain.
In our noble healing
With the courage to appeal—
An immortal story will be written.

***

Duty

The government has done its best, but we must fulfill the rest.
Negligence is not fair,
Wearing masks and keeping social distance–
Observe these measures with utmost care.

Let us embrace our responsibility,
And spread this message with clarity.
Follow appropriate behaviour as prevention,
Do not view them as an unwelcome restriction.
Negligence is not fair,
Wearing masks and keeping social distance–
Help dispel the clouds of despair.

Underestimating the enemy is a grave mistake,
Safety measures we cannot forsake.
We will win and continue to fight,
As brave soldiers in this battle of might.
Negligence is not fair,
Wearing masks and keeping social distance–
Help fight the pandemic with flair.

***

Responsibility

A new wave of Corona is rising, spreading through every part.

The threat looms large, both at home and outside,
Let us become wise and stop its spread far and wide.
Stay safe, wear masks, and keep two yards apart.

Recognise this as our final chance,
Avoid blaming others, and take a firm stance.
Children, elders, and youth—each must play their part.

Vaccines have arrived long-awaited,
Let us get everyone vaccinated.
Embrace your responsibility with a big heart.

***

Empathy

In times of global tragedy–
Empathy is nearly dead,
Even a deceased is treated here as a commodity.
Watching from afar,
Humanity stands helpless, and fears to tread.

Unlawful disbursal of medicine
or hoarding oxygen cylinder–
We find our hands stained with blood
At the display of such cruel behaviour.

A touch of compassion may still exist–
But it is overshadowed by the prevailing despair.
Empathy is nearly dead;
Even the deceased has become a business affair.

Death stood at our door
as we forsook the essence of life.
Exchanging diamonds for mere trinkets–
Ashamed as we are, defeated by strife.

A touch of compassion may still exist—
But it is overshadowed by the prevailing despair.
Empathy is nearly dead;
Even the deceased has become a business affair.

***

A Tale of Sanjeevani and Despair

Today, the pen is deeply distressed.
Rama is anxious,
The breath of his brother Lakshmana has reached a breaking point!

Deep gloom spans like a serpent-trap,
A veil of night snatches away gleam.
The world sleeps in profound despair–
The moment of celebration has become a dream.

Today, the pen is deeply distressed.
Rama is anxious,
The breath of his brother Lakshmana has reached a breaking point!

Hear the anguished cry of the wounded heart,
Echoing the sorrow in the mind with no escape.
Strength wanes with every effort, and folly prevails–
Now, death stands with its mouth agape.

Today, the pen is deeply distressed.
Rama is anxious,
The breath of his brother Lakshmana has reached a breaking point!

Every moment sees the frailty of age increase,
The breath of life becomes diminished.
Not even the courage of Jatayu can endure—
The elusive Sanjeevani herb has vanished.

Today, the pen is deeply distressed.
Rama is anxious,
The breath of his brother Lakshmana has reached a breaking point!

***

Identity

Every life is precious,
Every human is invaluable.

Medicine and doctors,
Oxygen cylinders,
Beds in the hospital,
And above all—
The desire for a vibrant life is truly priceless.
Every life is precious,
Every human is invaluable.

When in difficulty or shortage,
Let every heart hold the courage.
Fortune will embellish the crown—
His grace will surely pour down.
The God is anonymous, but
His recognizance is pure and viceless.
Every life is precious,
Every human is invaluable.

***

Vital Air

In this hour of crisis, O mind! Keep your patience.

> *Death dances everywhere,*
> *Leaving no limit behind.*
> *By fleeing from the truth,*
> *We become helpless and blind.*

> *If laziness has taken hold,*
> *Let today the truth unfold.*
> *In this hour of crisis, O mind! Keep your patience.*

> *Masks, social distancing of six feet,*
> *And vaccines well-conceived—*
> *Only through cooperation,*
> *Victory will be fully achieved.*

> *To reclaim eternity on the ground,*
> *Let us bring down the life profound.*
> *In this hour of crisis, O mind! Keep your patience.*

***

Examination

COVID is a harsh strife.
The world exists only with life.

Negligence in wearing masks,
And breaking social distance while doing tasks,
We invite the catastrophe
By provoking COVID for free.
To our utter dismay,
The smile on our faces has faded away.
COVID is a harsh strife.
The world exists only with life.

If you have a cough and fever—
Get tested at the hospital sooner.
Seek a timely prescription,
Hiding the illness is a bad decision.
Everyone is battling the pandemic,
Gripped in disbelief and panic.
COVID is a harsh strife.
The world exists only with life.

***

A Wake-Up Call

The conditions have turned quite dire,
Negligence has stained our hands with death's ire.
Had we not been careless in our plight,
We would have worn masks day and night.

And would have washed hands with flair–
We would not have mourned our loved ones in despair.
We shunned the vaccine with disdain–
But chew gutka and paan without any refrain.

We held ourselves high in arrogance,
Claiming invincibility sans allegiance.
In this spreading pandemic-grip,
We are vulnerable like a sinking ship.

The conditions have grown perilous indeed,
A moment of carelessness and death, we concede.

***

In Accord

To align with COVID-circumstance,
Let us adopt the right stance.
Wear masks and keep distance of two yards—
Embrace the practice, heed the guards.

If you seem slightly unwell—
With cough, fever or loss of smell,
Do keep a social distance,
And get tested soon for the first instance.

Follow what the doctor has to say,
Commence treatment without delay.
Consume nutritious food and ensure
That restful sleep is ample and pure.

Enhance immunity with milk and turmeric,
Practice yoga, meditation and music.
COVID-protocol, we must abide—
Let our behaviour reflect this guide.

Let clean air and gentle waters flow,
Let life sustain and grow.
When heartfelt gratitude to God and Nature is maintained,
Only then will our existence be sustained.

As per COVID's strictures, let us act—
With masks worn and social distancing intact.
Embrace greetings while keeping apart,
With respect and care in every heart.

***

Courage

Today, we need the courage to battle the plight,
To join hands with strength and might.
Blame is easy, but the solution is hard to find,
Let us have a look into the mind.

Let us pledge together, firm and true—
With body, mind, and wealth that we value.
Set aside pride, in victory or defeat,
Commit to service as a divine retreat.

The past is past, let it be, instead,
Let us focus together on what lies ahead.
Imbibe patience within your mind,
Unite in every task, never to look behind.

Shape our destiny with care and grace,
Ensure that nothing goes amiss in this race.
Today, we need courage to fight the strife,
To stand united and preserve our life.

***

Triumph through Adversity

The trial is harsh and rough,
But let not your spirit reach the trough.
Even if death stands plainly in view,
Let the desire for life remain within your purview.

Though some pearls may break,
And loved ones may leave in the wake—
Let hope sprout from the core of despair,
And grow tall, braving the storms, unfair.

Hold firm to your courage, no matter how tough,
When the stream of destiny stream is harsh enough.
The trial is harsh and rough,
But let not your spirit reach the trough.

How long will the darkness gather and loom?
It will soon scatter into the gloom.
Through the fire test, we shall emerge,
Like glittering gold, with resilience to surge.

Even if the waters flow against our stride,
Let our resolve soar high with pride.
Even if death stands plainly in view,
Let the desire for life remain within your purview.

***

Dark Days

These days are difficult and dark,
But soon, the sky will have a spark.
We will triumph over COVID one day,
And the shadows will fade away.

The dawn will break the gloom,
And joy will fill every room.
Fear and doubt will no longer reign,
Humanity has set off on a campaign.

The trial we face today–
It will eventually give way.
The mind will be free again,
Divinity we shall attain.

With a new vigour daily,
The life will sparkle brightly.
Nightingale will sing the melody,
In celebration and remedy.

Do not let the values decay
And the human life go astray.
These dark days will transform,
And brighter days will reform.

***

Gift of Fearlessness

Where there is a problem, a solution will arise,
A night is a dawn in disguise.

Though the boat is small and the current strong,
We will find the shore where we belong.
Even if the Iron Gate is shut tight,
Victory belongs to those who do not lose sight.
After the silent night, songs will surprise,
Where there is a problem, a solution will arise.

Even ice starts to melt with courage,
And barren lands yield oil, says the adage.
In thorns, no one else can dwell—
But the brave souls succeed with no yell.
Where there is fear, let divine grace realise,
Where there is a problem, a solution will arise.

***

Sacrifices for Safety

More precious than our own lives
Is to ensure that humanity thrives.

Every day, we make an oblation
To guard our motherland from invasion.

Today, we face a daunting time,
In a battle against a pandemic prime.

Some are ill, their health in disarray,
Others have lost their lives along the way.

With medicines scarce and oxygen plight,
We strive to make everything right.

More precious than our own lives
Is to ensure that humanity thrives.

We shall strive, what we can achieve,
We will not fear the battle and leave.

We will conquer death and become victorious
To hold the crown of life glorious.

We will establish a world anew,
With healing, peace, and hope in view.

More precious than our own lives
Is to ensure that humanity thrives.

***

Healing

Let no more waves of sorrow rise,
May we let go of the suffering and be wise!
Let joy paint every corner bright,
And healing grace be our sight.

The times of ruin have slipped away,
Brave warriors stand their ground, come what may.
Let the dark dealings and extortion cease,
May justice reign and bring us peace.

When the battle is for the life to sustain,
May the death not wreak havoc again.
Let joy adorn each passing day,
Let the healing light guide our way.

No one shall be bereaved or homeless,
May every need be met with progress.
Let education be our constant guide,
Let truth and fairness be on our side.

May deceit and falsehood fade away,
And truth remain unshattered, stay.
Let joy fill every corner bright,
And healing grace be our sight.

***

Empowered Triumph

Victory over COVID lies in our grip,
If we do not let our determination slip.
Wear your mask and keep your distance—
Adhere to these with persistence.

The virus is tiny, that brings dismay,
But medical science has found a way.
We can control the infection outright
With vaccines and treatments now in sight.

Recognise symptoms before they advance,
And act swiftly in the first instance.
Victory over COVID lies in our grip,
If we do not let our determination slip.

Manage diabetes and hypertension with care,
Swift control is necessary; be aware.
Ample rest, pure food, yoga and meditation—
Change the lifestyle for primary prevention.

Nothing is beyond reach if unitedly we stand—
With divine blessings, we will command.
Victory over COVID lies in our grip,
If we do not let our determination slip.

***

Blessed Guardians

On the path of service, always ready,
Setting aside selfishness, staying steady,
Writing a new chapter with care—
We are the COVID warriors, strong and rare.

Piercing through darkness deep,
As the monsoon rains begin to seep,
With enlightened minds and bodies pure,
We are nature's stole for cure.

No doubts or fears in our way,
With compassion, we brighten each day.
We are the cool, calm breeze in desolate,
Guardians of peace in the chaotic state.

With joyous hearts and nurturing hands,
Abundant blessings across the lands,
We are the bearers of tranquil joy—
Guardians we are, wellness we deploy.

***

Awakening Awareness

We will awaken the public's mind,
And encourage all to get aligned.
No more waves of trouble should return,
We will drive out COVID with measures stern.

Let us ensure safety for the common man,
And strengthen defences with a thoughtful plan.
Successful vaccination will pave the way
To make the battle easier day by day.

Let everyone be informed,
And awareness be brainstormed–
Avoiding deceit and false flair,
Dismissing the myths and despair.

Let us not fall into a trap,
And march ahead with a clear map.
We will clear confusion and dismay,
Awaken wisdom, light the way.

***

Eid of Hope

May Each Soul Revel in Eid's blessing,
Stay blessed with the hope of living.

Wearing masks and keeping distance,
May this reminder bring persistence,
May He bestow peace and prudence–
May Each Soul Revel in Eid's blessing,
Stay blessed with the hope of living.

Fear, anguish and pain are rife,
Brave warriors battle for life,
Our divine duty amid the strife–
May Each Soul Revel in Eid's blessing,
Stay blessed with the hope of living.

May healing alleviate the pain,
May allegiance defeat disdain.
May we turn every loss into gain–
May Each Soul Revel in Eid's Blessing,
Stay blessed with the hope of living.

***

Heavenly Triumph

In the glow of the full moon's gleam,
Every corner will shimmer and beam.
Victory will come, serene and clear,
And COVID's shadow will disappear.
The world will triumph over the disease,
And COVID will meet its defeat with ease.

By forming a robust safety screen,
Wearing masks and getting the vaccine,
Embracing two yards of space,
And keeping hands clean with grace—
The world will triumph over the disease,
And COVID will meet its defeat with ease.

With discipline as your guide,
Embrace breath and yoga wide.
Forge a body pure and bright—
Like gold refined by firelight.
The world will triumph over the disease,
And COVID will meet its defeat with ease.

As the sun dispels the night,
Our spirits will rise to a new height.
The pandemic has taken the world hostage,
Sow the seeds of creation with brimful courage.
The world will triumph over the disease,
And COVID will meet its defeat with ease.

Every class divide is but a façade,
Life offers equality, unscarred.
Where actions are free and unbound,
Heavenly realms touch the ground.
The world will triumph over the disease,
And COVID will meet its defeat with ease.

***

Battle of Resolve

Wear the mask, keep two yards apart–
Until we resolve in the heart.
The truth is plain, and we are not unaware–
The battle is tough, beyond compare.

The virus always keeps interfering,
Its shape continually re-appearing,
Playing indeed a dreadful game,
The pen fails to describe the same.

We are not naive to the fact,
The struggle is far from a simple act.
Let no new wave come too near,
May every town and village steer clear.

Let death not bring its wrath and fear,
And no lives be lost in vain, anywhere.
Avoid careless displays and dismay,
Leave no room for neglect or delay.

Healing is what we desire,
Do not let aspirations fall to the fire.
The truth is plain, and we are not unaware—
The battle is tough, beyond compare.

***

Vaccination

The disease will not grip us tight,
If immunization is done right.
Embrace the shots with ardent zeal,
Build defences for the body to heal.

There are no grave side effects to fear,
Night will pass, and dawn is near.
Prepare for triumph; go and grab,
Let no person miss the jab.

Let no deceit, nor fear, nor spite,
Fill our minds with fright.
Embrace the shots with ardent zeal,
Build defences for the body to heal.

Covaxin has been made at home with pride,
Covishield, too, has moved with stride.
Sputnik has also received permission,
Vaccination is a voluntary mission.

May the health of people be bright,
With energy and vigour, pure delight.
Embrace the shots with ardent zeal,
Build defences for the body to heal.

***

Slaves to Our Own Delusions

Whether it is COVID or 'Black Fungus,'
How helpless is humanity in its fuss!

Caught in the web of endless desires,
Ensnared by itself, it still conspires.

With amassed wealth and fortune unbound,
Desire grows for no reason sound.

In the fire, it ignites so close and dire,
It scorches itself, consumed by its pyre.

Today, enslaved by the cruel game of time,
It yearns for moments, fleeting and slime.

***

Fear

Who knows what curse, what fear's design
Has turned this pandemic into a dire sign!

In grave ignorance, humanity falls,
Embracing death, heedless of the calls.

No mask worn; no crowd controlled–
Letting the reckless story unfold.

In false pride, we miss the truth upright,
Lost in sleep, oblivious to the plight.

A stumble shattered our dreams–
No petals are there to greet, only thorns and screams.

Worsened conditions, who knows the curse?
What a fearsome scene, so adverse!

***

Victory Call

Hold on to your courage now, dear friend!
Victory will be ours in the end.

The dark spell of sorrow will cease,
A new dawn will bring us ease.

Masks and distancing are a must,
Vaccination is another area of thrust.

No more scenes of death and doom,
Let there be no misery or gloom or gloom.

Let us not stray from the war,
Victory for humanity is not so far.

Hold on to your courage now, dear friend!
Victory will be ours in the end.

The battle with the pandemic is tough,
Measures taken by us are not enough.

However, our resolve is strong and bold,
Soon, joyful cheers will unfold.

We will define the date of conquest,
For the just cause, full of zest.

Hold on to your courage now, dear friend!
Victory will be ours in the end.

***

Navigating Crisis with Grace

In this hour of trial, let patience guide your mind.

Embrace pure food and conduct with care,
Practice yoga and breathing with mindful prayer.
With a heart purified by wisdom's light,
sing sweetly with love, your spirit bright.

Rise with the dawn, and may a restful sleep you find!

Quit the betel, tobacco and wine,
Anger, envy and ego are not divine.
Embrace self-control, service and sacrifice,
Nurture your soul and forsake the vice.

With steadfast resolve, victory you will find.

***

Epiphany

Such a simple truth, yet so elusive,
The mind could be more decisive.

Wearing masks and keeping a distance—
Such a humble appeal meets resistance.

The dark days full of grief have elapsed,
When the lives we adored collapsed.

Chaos and wails filled the air,
Oxygen was a scarce affair.

Even when all measures fell short,
Resistance was not sought.

Wearing masks and keeping a distance—
Such a humble appeal meets resistance.

Everyone was lost in regret,
Haunted by nightmares, difficult to forget.

No glimmer of hope shone bright,
Death and agony were a constant blight.

Reflecting on those harsh times of yore,
We have neither remorse nor sore.

Wearing masks and keeping a distance—
Such a humble appeal meets resistance.

Everyone wandered lost in sorrow,
Nightmares clouded our tomorrow.

No ray of hope shone through the gloom,
A shadow loomed as a certain doom.

Reflecting on those days of dread,
No anger stirs in the heart instead.

Wearing masks and keeping a distance—
Such a humble appeal meets resistance.

***

Witness

A handful of light dispels the dark,
Truth prevails, and lies disembark—
Witnessed by the world through ages as a spark.

Even after a stark moonless night,
The dawn will rise with all its might.
The radiance of truth is pure and bright—
A new beginning beyond death's sight.
A handful of light dispels the dark,
Truth prevails, and lies disembark—
Witnessed by the world through ages as a spark.

Even if shrouded by clouds of hopelessness,
Let the heart stay firm within, and do not egress.
No doubt the pain will cease,
Just a few days until the release.
A handful of light dispels the dark,
Truth prevails, and lies disembark—
Witnessed by the world through ages as a spark.

***

Salutation

We once lit lamps with hope—
Let us not allow the light to fade!
Flowers showered from the sky—
Let not a single bloom wither away!

The heroes of the pandemic—
Doctors, nurses, and the brave forces majestic
Have each served with passion newborn,
In every house, garlands of praise adorn.

We once lit lamps with hope—
Let us not allow the light to fade!

With empty bellies and dry lips,
From head to toe, the sweat that drips—
They taught us the strength to face,
And how to live and serve with grace.

They have healed wounds of humanity,
With loving care amid calamity.

We once lit lamps with hope–
Let us not allow the light to fade!

***

www.ingramcontent.com/pod-product-compliance
Lightning Source LLC
LaVergne TN
LVHW041541070526
838199LV00046B/1771